THE HALF LIFE OF A YOGURT COATED RAISIN

R Campbell Zaino

DEDICATION

For Mum and Dad

CONTENTS

She Turns Away

Did You Write the Book of Love?

HALF LIFE

I have a vase of flowers

that are half dead.

A clock on the wall
that is an hour slow.

A bottle of wine
that is half empty.

Candles
that are burnt out.

This is life.
My life.
The half life
that nobody sees.

The half life
that is just me.

The half life
That I like.

UNACCEPTABLE APOLOGY

(My most (in)sincer apologies)

Oh good God!

It's a horror.

Someone call for help,

this girl is thinking for herself!

Someone really should tell her

that it's really not on,

that when they pull on the lead

she should follow.

She's being so radical,

it's just not logical.

She's so cynical,

it's diabolical.

I'm sorry I'm being so radical,

unlogical,

cynical,

and diabolical,

but it's not my fault.

You see I was brought up wrong,

without your lack of vision.

I know you're respectable,

and I'm unpredictable.

I know that my cynicism is cheap,

and that's why I'm making this apology

so tongue in cheek.

THE PIGEON LOFT

The men in the suits want you to play by their rules.

They want you to fit in the establishment groove.

You must do as they say
(But not as they do).

There can't be any exception to the rules.

You must follow their lead
and not think for yourself.

They'll call you a rebel,
if you break the bureaucracy mould.

But above all you must be able to be pigeonholed.
Well, have I got news for you?

This little pigeon
won't fit
in your hole.

IN THE LION'S DEN

I always know where you'll be
so I sit there long enough,
and you come to me.

And in that moment,
I'm in the limelight of your eyes
I'm in Nirvana
I've won every prize.

Then you dart away
and I'm left to watch,
you work the room.
like the moon works the clocks.

And in that moment,
It all becomes clear
trying to hold you down,
is like trying to catch the wind
with a spear.

LOVE IS NOT A MATHEMATICAL EQUATION

Love is not a mathematical equation.
It can not be measured
or calculated.

There is no square root,
no prime number,
no common denominator.

Love is a variable,
ever fluctuating,
always changing.

Love is spontaneous.
Combustible.
Immeasurable.

Love is not a mathematical equation.

I REALISED I WAS

I realised I was
not am,
but was.

I didn't see it in myself
until I saw it in another child's eyes
full of tears.
The word
lonely
hanging in every drop.

I tried to help
dried the eyes,
encouraged a smile.
Because that's what I do
not because it's my role,
but because it called
to my soul.

And that's when

I realised I was
not am,
but was.

WORK THOUGHTS
FROM A BED

I can't sleep
because I can't sleep, she said.
I smiled
I shouldn't have, she didn't mean it as a joke
but it reminded me of some long forgotten recent work
where people speak their minds
in beautiful unrhythmic rhyme.
Rhythm
Helps
Your
Two
Hips
Move
They teach the kids at school
but I can't bring the mnemonic to mind
so the recent work goes long forgotten
drops into the hubbub of my brain
and mingles with
the sleepless woman
the rhythm kids
the rhyming slang.
The Big Bang
and Christian beliefs
girls flower names and boys grazed knees
and all the other things I think of when
I can't sleep.

LIFE AS A YOGHURT COATED RAISIN

It's all a question of taste,
I don't see what's so good about cola cubes,
and liquorice lace.
Or banana whirls
And sherbet spaceships.

There's no question that sugared
almonds are their favourites
with their hard centre,
and their pretty coloured,
candy sweet casing.
They buy them straight away,
without hesitating.

But nobody wants me.
They don't like my tangy hard shell,
and soft sweet centre.
That's why I'm always left here
the last jar on the shelf
of the candy store counter.

IVORY TOWERS

You're so bloody perfect,
Aren't you?
You on the estate.
With your mock Tudor houses,
and manicured nails.
You have your holidays in Florida,
The Sunshine State,
with your two point four children.
and designer names.
Everything's so bloody wonderful
in your ivory towers.
You'll go on thinking that this is real life,
till you're covered in flowers.

WE FORGET

We think we're busy,
we think we're stressed,
we think our life is a long one-way road
and we've taken a wrong turn.

We worry about money,
we complain about work.
We judge our life by
a fake, manufactured world.

But we forget
that we lay our heads on a warm, comfy bed.
We have food,
we have shelter,
we have love.

We forget
to listen to the bird's song,
the sound of the rain, the purr of the cat.

We forget
how much we really have.

OPENED

A lifetime opened
with a click
of a switch.
Memories
fall like rain against my mind's window.
Pain, in some
laughter in lots.
Ghosts of lives
of lovers lost
friends forgotten
but burning bright.
Memories
splashing like kids in puddles.
Some blurred around the edges
but still not deleted.
A portal to the past.
A lifetime opened.

THERE, BUT
NOT HERE

(For Dad)

A shadow
of a man
there, but not here.

A wholly ghost
of the father
and the son.

Not her husband,
not our Dad.

There, but not here.

A soul taken
before the body
of the man he used to be.

Like the ticking of a clock
or the beat of a drum,
he was there.
but now he's not here.

HEAVEN'S HEART
(Dedicated to the memory of Tony Steele.)

Where do we go when we die?
If heaven's so beautiful,
Why do people cry?
Where do we go when we die?
How can we cease to exist
when we live on in a loved one's mind?
Where do we go when we die?
Do we just rot in the earth,
nothing more than mortal bone?
Where do we go when we die?
Does heaven exist,
or has it all been one long lie?
Where do we go when we die?
We all go to heaven,
because heaven exists in someone's heart.

WHAT NO ONE TELLS YOU ABOUT DEATH

This is what no one tells you about death

you have to go on living.

You have to go to the supermarket

and buy

cat food

tea Bags

toilet Rolls.

You have to get death certificates.

Meet undertakers.

Choose flowers,

and readings,

and songs.

You have to feed the cat,

wash your hair,

and the dishes,

You have to go on living.

And that's what no one tells you

about death.

THE SILENT SLEEP NO MORE

Awake.
The silent sleep no more.
No dreams
no rest
they have a tale to tell.
And the silent shall sleep no more.
Stolen lives of stolen love
babes from the arms of maids
taken in trust
to shadowy graves.
But now they are awake
and the guilty must pay.
For the silent shall sleep no more.

WHERE ONLY HOPE REMAINS

A box has been opened
and slowly
over the weeks,
months,
years
all confidence
has been worn away.

Now only hope remains.

Hope
that there is something
more

Hope
that there will be light
in darkness

Hope
that I'll beat this canker
that is eating
all
hope
away

The box in my soul has been opened
And only
A little

Hope
Remains

SHE TURNS AWAY

She turned away
too quickly.
She did want to let her see
pretended to be reading Joyce of Keats.
Dracula
that seemed appropriate.
Gothic flesh
inappropriate
lust.

DID YOU WRITE THE BOOK OF LOVE?

(Found text poem using the lyrics of
American Pie by Don Mclean and
She Bop by Stephen Broughton Lunt, Cyndi
Lauper, Richard Chertoff, Gary S Cohen)

Can you teach me how
to make those people dance
like them good old boys
in tight blue jeans?

Do you recall what was revealed?
I met a girl who sang the blues
and I've been thinking of a new sensation
but she just smiled and turned away.

A voice that came
says I better stop,
but I won't worry,
and I won't fret,
ain't no law against it yet.
The courtroom was adjourned,
no verdict was returned.

I can't remember if I cried,
but something touched me deep inside,
so,
"bye-bye, Miss American Pie
drove my Chevy to the levee
but the levee was dry.
Them good old boys were drinking whiskey and rye
singing, "This'll be the day that I die."

This will be the day that I die"

ABOUT THE AUTHOR

R Campbell Zaino

Born and raised in York, UK R (Rachel) Campbell Zaino is a poet and author whose work has been published in the UK, USA, and Australia.

Rachel has a BA(hons) degree in Theatre, Film and Television, and a Masters degree in Creative Writing.

Printed in Great Britain
by Amazon

83789095R10020